THE GOLDEN GOAL

For Shannon, Nathan and Thomas—M.C.
For Mozzarella—P.G.

The Golden Goal
Text copyright © 2020 by Matthew Cade.
Illustrations copyright © 2020 by Patrick Gray.

First edition.

Published by Collins, an imprint of HarperCollins Publishers Ltd.

HarperCollins books may be purchased for educational, business,
or sales promotional use through our Special Markets Department.

HarperCollins Publishers Ltd
Bay Adelaide Centre, East Tower
22 Adelaide Street West, 41st Floor
Toronto, Ontario, Canada
M5H 4E3

www.harpercollins.ca

Library and Archives Canada Cataloguing in Publication

Title: The golden goal / Matthew Cade ; Illustrated by Patrick Gray.
Names: Cade, Matthew, author. | Gray, Patrick, 1984- illustrator.
Identifiers: Canadiana (print) 20200288717 | Canadiana (ebook) 20200288725
ISBN 9781443463393 (hardcover) | ISBN 9781443463409 (ebook)
Subjects: LCSH: Olympic Winter Games (21st : 2010 : Vancouver, B.C.)—Juvenile literature.
LCSH: Hockey—Canada—History—21st century—Juvenile literature.
Classification: LCC GV848.4.C3 C33 2020 | DDC j796.962/66—dc23

Printed and bound in the United States of America.
PHX 10 9 8 7 6 5 4 3 2 1

THE GOLDEN GOAL

BY MATTHEW CADE   ILLUSTRATED BY PATRICK GRAY

CANADA

Collins
N IMPRINT OF HARPERCOLLINS PUBLISHERS LTD

ON AN OVERTIME GOAL FROM THE STICK OF THE KID: TWENTY-TWO-YEAR-OLD COLE HARBOUR NATIVE NAMED SID.

THE CANADIAN ROSTER WAS STACKED TO THE BRIM,

PLAYERS WITH PASSION AND VIGOUR AND VIM.

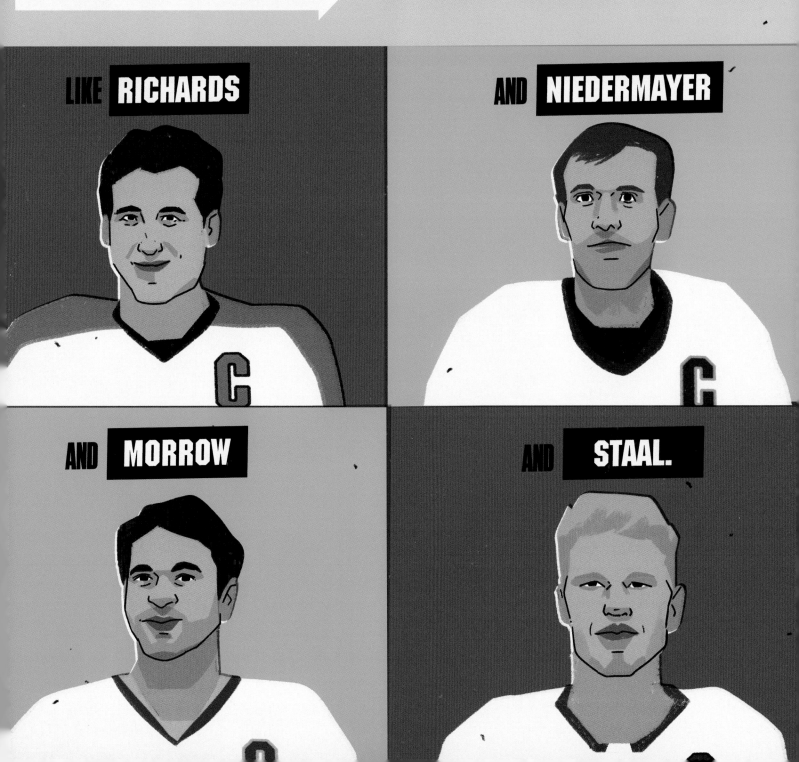

WITH

BOYLE

CANADA

AND

SEABROOK

CANADA

AND

DOUGHTY

CANADA

AND

PRONGER.

CANADA

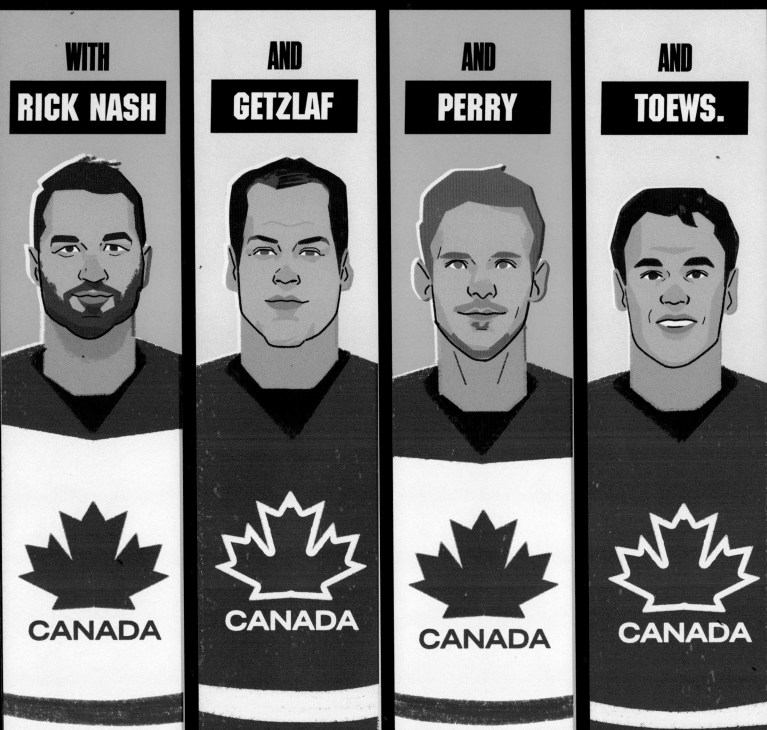

WITH
RICK NASH

AND
GETZLAF

AND
PERRY

AND
TOEWS.

CANADA

CANADA

CANADA

CANADA

93 ALL STAR

SIDNEY CROSBY

**"GENERATIONAL," THEY SAID,
THE BEST SINCE LEMIEUX,
ALREADY COMPARED
TO THE GAME'S CHOSEN FEW.**

BUT NOT 'TIL VANCOUVER AND THE GOLD MEDAL GAME

DID SIDNEY ASCEND BEYOND TYPICAL FAME.

WHEN HE SCORED, ACROSS CANADA EVERYONE KNEW:

NO GOAL MORE IMPORTANT SINCE '72.

PERRY
7:13 - 2ND PERIOD
ASSISTS: GETZLAF, KEITH

TOEWS
12:50 - 1ST PERIOD
ASSIST: RICHARDS

CANADA

CANADA

THE GAME WAS PLAYED AT AN INCREDIBLE SPEED, AND CANADA JUMPED OUT TO A 2-0 LEAD.

KESLER
12:44 - 2ND PERIOD
ASSIST: KANE

BUT BACK CAME THE US TO RUIN THE FUN, AND AFTER TWO PERIODS, THE SCORE WAS 2-1.

THEN, LATE IN THE THIRD, IT WAS ZACH PARISE, WHO TIED IT AT TWO WITH JUST SECONDS TO PLAY.

SO, TO OVERTIME THEY WENT, THUS SETTING THE STAGES FOR A FANTASTIC FINISH, AND ONE FOR THE AGES.

THE ICE WAS WIDE OPEN,
THEY PLAYED FOUR ON FOUR.

THE TEAMS TRADED CHANCES,
BOTH DESPERATE TO SCORE.

THEN, WITH TWELVE AND A HALF TO GO IN O.T.,
KID CROSBY ATTACKED ONE ON FOUR, FORCEFULLY...

LOST THE PUCK IN THE CORNER, WHEN IT BUMPED THE REF'S SKATE,
A SMALL, HAPPY ACCIDENT, A MOMENT OF FATE.

WITH THE "D" RIGHT ON TOP OF HIM, AN IDEA STRUCK:

CROSBY SAW IGINLA AND POKED HIM THE PUCK.

AND THE SOUND OF IT ROSE ABOVE THE DIN OF THE CROWD,
BOLD AND CONFIDENT, FEARLESS AND LOUD.

IT RATTLED
OFF THE RAFTERS
AND ECHOED
OFF THE BEAMS,
ONE WORD—
CROSBY'S VOICE.

12:22
2   OVERTIME   2

"IGGY!
HE SCREAMED.

AND FASTER THAN YOU COULD BLINK,
NOT A SECOND BUT A FRACTION,

CROSBY SHOT THE PUCK BEFORE MILLER REACTED.

IT SLIPPED THROUGH HIS PADS
AND LIKE THAT IT WAS DONE,
THE COUNTRY ERUPTED—

CANADA HAD WON!

THE LAST DAY OF THE GAMES, THE FINAL EVENT,
FANS BARELY BREATHING, THEIR ENERGY SPENT,

THEY NOW COULD EXHALE AND BASK IN THE GLOW
OF THE GOLDEN GOAL FROM CROSBY, A CANADIAN HERO.